STORES
and RETAIL
SPACES

six

ST MEDIA GROUP
INTERNATIONAL
CINCINNATI, OHIO

ISBN: 0-944094-49-X

PUBLISHED BY:

ST Books
ST Media Group International Inc.
407 Gilbert Avenue
Cincinnati, Ohio 45202
Tel. 513-421-2050 • Fax 513-421-6110
E-mail: books@stmediagroup.com
www.stmediagroup.com/stbooks

DISTRIBUTED TO THE U.S. BOOK AND ART TRADE BY:

Watson-Guptill Publications
770 Broadway
New York, NY 10003
www.watsonguptill.com

DISTRIBUTED OUTSIDE THE U.S. TO THE BOOK AND ART TRADE BY:

Harper Design International
10 East 53rd Street
New York, NY 10022
www.harpercollins.com/hdi

Book design by Kim Pegram, Art Director, *VM+SD*

Book written and edited by Carole Winters, Associate Publisher, *VM+SD;* Steve Kaufman, Editor, *VM+SD;*
Matt Hall, Managing Editor, *VM+SD;* Anne DiNardo, Associate Editor, *VM+SD;* Alicia Hanson, Associate Editor, *VM+SD*

Printed in China
10 9 8 7 6 5 4 3 2 1

STORES
and RETAIL
SPACES

s i x

**From the Institute of Store Planners and
the Editors of *VM+SD* magazine**

For 33 years, and counting, retail designers and contract architect/design firms

have submitted their finest projects to be judged by a jury of their peers –

members of the Institute of Store Planners, the recognized organization of

professional store planners and designers dedicated to excellence in the devel-

opment of retail environments.

**Here on display are the winners in the
2003 ISP/VM+SD International Store Design Competition.**

Store of the Year

First Place

Awards of Merit

Store of the Year Winner

Aveda Tokyo Lifestyle Salon and Spa
Tokyo

FRCH Design Worldwide, Cincinnati

Aesthetics and environmentalism share equal billing throughout the Aveda Tokyo Lifestyle Salon and Spa, this year's ISP/VM+SD Store of the Year. The 3-story, 6000-square-foot prototype represents Aveda's first foray into the Japanese market, and is the result of a three-year collaboration by FRCH Design Worldwide (Cincinnati), Aveda's in-house design team in New York and the Tokyo-based retail store development team at Aveda's parent company, Estée Lauder.

Designers say the shop/salon/spa/café is a physical representation of Aveda's corporate philosophy, as articulated by founder Horst Rechelbacher: "Our mission is to care for the world we live in, from the products we make to the ways in which we give back to society. At Aveda, we strive to set an example of environmental leadership and responsibility, not just in the world of beauty but also around the world."

In keeping with those ideals, fixtures and furniture throughout the Tokyo salon are made with Tamo oak, a locally sourced wood that's harvested to control soil erosion. Other "green" touches within the space include: flooring and stairs made of Sokoita wood that was reclaimed from a demolished, century-old farm-

house; cabinets made from compressed corn sorghum stalks; walls finished in low VOC (volatile organic compound) paints that are non-toxic and non-polluting; and solar panels on the roof that partially power the spa's operations.

Jan Tribbey, Aveda's vp, planning and design, notes that the emphasis on the natural extends to the building's lighting. "The front of the building is all glass, and the rear is at least 30 percent glass," Tribbey notes. "That reduces the space's reliance on artificial light. Also, natural light is best for customers when it comes to viewing the hair-color processing and other services offered by the salon."

CLIENT Aveda, New York – Chris Hacker, senior vp, global marketing & design; Jan Tribbey, vp, planning and design; Monroe Alechman, vp, visual merchandising; Sojiro Inoue, retail design director, Tokyo

DESIGN FRCH Design Worldwide, Cincinnati – James Lazzari, partner; Andrew McQuilkin, vp/creative director; Jay Kratz, design director; Lori Kolthoff, director, resource design; Frank Liebgott, project architect; Franck Steinglen, designer; Jeff Waggoner, graphic production director

ARCHITECT Heart, Tokyo – Masao Murakami, project architect

PHOTOGRAPHY Nacasa & Partners, Tokyo

First Place Winners

Lotte Department Store
Daegu Station, South Korea
FRCH Design Worldwide, Cincinnati

Reinforcing its position as the leading retailer in South Korea, Lotte Department Store opened a 12-level, 750,000-square-foot, full-line store in Daegu, one of the country's fastest-growing cities.

Far more elegant than previous Lotte stores, the crisp interiors create a fresh, contemporary backdrop for the retailer's extensive merchandise collection. Designed as a destination for a full day of shopping, the store includes a youth zone, international fresh food market and food court, restaurants, spa and movie theaters.

An overall unifying design concept allows the flexibility to meet the store's diverse customer profile while maintaining the consistency of the Lotte brand.

The "Lotte Jewel Box" concept enables the design style to flow and adjust freely from floor to floor while reintroducing and repeating common themes.

Built over a subway station, the store's architectural design includes a pedestrian plaza surrounding the store; a five-level attached garage; and two levels of direct access to subway transportation.

CLIENT Lotte Department Store, Seoul – Kyuk-Ho Shin, chairman; In-Won Lee, president; Hee-Tae Kang, gm, merchandise strategy; Jun Jang, chief designer; Hyeong-Se Soe, senior project designer; Kil-Yong Park, design director; Bo Sang Park, Hoe-Dong Yeo, senior designers; Byung Yong Nho, managing director, sales division; Won-Woon Lee, planning director; Byung-Muk Jung, director; Jong-Yun Oh, Jeong-Won Hong, designers

DESIGN FRCH Design Worldwide, Cincinnati – Jim Lazzari, principal-in-charge/partner; Andrew McQuilkin, vp, design; Young Rok Park, senior designer; Dan Mayzum, project manager; Jeanine Storn, design director; Raejean Downs, Heesun Kim, Frank Stenglein, designers; Lori Kolthoff, resource design director; Jim Fitzgerald Jr., planner

PHOTOGRAPHY Courtesy of Lotte Department Store, Seoul

STORES and RETAIL SPACES

DFS Galleria
Singapore

Callison Architecture Inc., Seattle

DFS Galleria wanted to become more than a store; it wanted to be a true tourist destination that captured the local flavor of each market in which it was located.

So a baseline prototype had to be created, over which the "local wonder" concept could be laid. An atmosphere for hospitality would differentiate it from just another general merchandise store. Additionally, each floor would have a unique environment that focused on the lifestyle the merchandise represented.

Since most customers are brought to the new Singapore store by bus, they are taken on a non-stop escalator ride from the ground floor to the fourth level and work their way back down. (It's the single longest escalator in Singapore.)

The fourth level is the Jungle Garden – representative of Singapore, the "Garden City" – and its natural materials, palette and plant selection create the feeling of walking outdoors.

Going down from there, the third level is Colonial Singapore, luxury merchandise presented in an environment reminiscent of Singapore's bygone history. Dark wood, white stucco, colonial-style furniture and light, airy space poignantly remember the elegant "black and white" architecture period.

Second is Modern Singapore and the street level represents Singapura – everything the city has to offer, including street vendors.

CLIENT DFS Galleria, Singapore

DESIGN Callison Architecture Inc., Seattle – Martin Anderson, principal-in-charge; Song Pak, project manager

PHOTOGRAPHY Chris Eden, Seattle

Hotel Collection by Charter Club
Macy's Herald Square, New York
Federated Merchandising Group, New York

The challenge was to develop a luxury bedding concept for a new private label. And the launch was Hotel Collection by Charter Club, developed by Federated Department Stores' Merchandising Group.

Perimeter wall fixturing houses solid programs in all the varying size ranges. The tops of the fixtures are merchandised with a touch of visual treatment. The use of frosted glass introduces a small logo to brand the fixtures. A Hotel "H" monogram is incorporated into the guardrail.

Floor fixtures consist of a combination product and presentation system, with built-in signholders. The customer is able to see the mixture of bedding components and coordinated sheets and to touch and feel the product. Lockable glass towers house the finest-quality fabrics.

Low-rise contemporary beds were incorporated for a residential touch, and built-in capacity shelving was incorporated in the rear of the headboard. Three-tiered bedside tables present bath, body and tabletop items. Bed placquard signholders, branded with an etched "H" monogram on the base, provide price and product information.

CLIENT Federated Merchandising Group, New York – Joe Feczko, executive vp; Ron Bausman, vp, visual and shop development; Rick Bolenis, visual manager; Young de Charette, shop design director; Brian Ford, shop development director

SUPPLIERS Artitalia Group, Montreal (fixtures); Bentley Mills Inc., City of Industry, Calif. (flooring); Adco Signs Inc., New York (signage)

PHOTOGRAPHY Ricky Zehavi, Brooklyn, N.Y.

Seibu Accessories Plus
Shibuya District, Tokyo

Callison Architecture Inc., Seattle

Seibu, one of Japan's largest department store retailers, was looking to create an accessories department that appealed to young, trendy customers.

From a design standpoint, it had to be changeable, tactile and touchable, with visual excitement and interest.

The Accessories Plus department created by Seibu and Callison (Seattle) has more cutting-edge style than the rest of the store's accessories department, demonstrated by the mosaic tile wall and handcrafted display tables (for which a bent sheetmetal base is cut with an organic pattern), accent flooring and lighting, presenting off-the-rack fashion accessories but with an illusion of exclusivity.

A series of low showcases snaking along a promenade can be shopped from both sides. These "play stations" are modeled like a vanity that invites customers to try on accessories.

A column fixture is designed with a random mix of backlit colored, frosted acrylic panels. Grid panels focus on accessories "stories," such as a display cube that can be merchandised like a collection.

CLIENT Millennium Development Co. – Masao Fujikawa, general manager, design planning division; Kaoru Matsumoto; project manager, design planning division; Seibu Department Store, Tokyo – Toshiaki Matsuhashi, environmental space and store planning, chief manager.

DESIGN Callison Architecture Inc., Seattle – Dawn Clark, principal; Elizabeth Buxton, Bryan Gailey, design; Joel Reihl, architecture

ARCHITECTURAL CONSULTANT The Earth Associates, Tokyo

SUPPLIERS Benjamin Moore, Tokyo (ceiling paint); Design Within Reach, Tokyo (furnishings); Yoshichu, Kyoto, Japan (fixtures); Sophia Inc., Tokyo (flooring, mosaic tile); Parco Space Systems, Tokyo (lighting)

PHOTOGRAPHY Chris Eden, Seattle

Patronik Designs Jewelry Gallery
Burlingame, Calif.

Miroglio Architecture + Design, Oakland, Calif.

Patronik Designs Jewelry Gallery houses both a jeweler's workshop studio and the work of owner/jeweler Nick Kosturos, who hoped to express his store's uniqueness as a place where his art is both viewed and sold.

Miroglio Architecture + Design (Oakland, Calif.) conceived the new space as a "prequel" to the former space (recently destroyed by fire), what would have been revealed if the walls of the previous space had been removed. Elements that were only suggested, or were two-dimensional, could now be articulated in three-dimensional form.

The store's form is an amalgamation of three distinct "ideals" that comprise the jeweler's image of himself: a "white box" art gallery forming the overall framework; an ancient reliquary or catacomb where precious items are stored (manifested in the reliquary wall in the center of the store that leans in like the side of a cave wall and features custom display fixtures within the niches); and a jeweler's workshop in the rear of the gallery.

All the suspended light fixtures in the store were custom-designed and handcrafted for the space by a local artisan.

CLIENT Patronik Designs Jewelry Gallery, Burlingame, Calif. – Nick Kosturos, ceo

DESIGN Miroglio Architecture + Design, Oakland, Calif. – Joel Miroglio, principal/design; Patrick Ahearn, associate

GENERAL CONTRACTOR Russell Nobles Construction, Santa Rosa, Calif.

SUPPLIERS USG, Chicago (ceiling); RNC, Santa Rosa, Calif. (fixtures); Atlas Carpet, City of Commerce, Calif. (flooring); Neidhardt Production, Half Moon Bay, Calif. (lighting); A Better Image, Castro Valley, Calif. (signage)

PHOTOGRAPHY Joel Gardner Photography, Oakland, Calif.

Futuretronics
Mall at Millenia, Orlando
Miroglio Architecture + Design, Oakland, Calif.

Futuretronics wanted to differentiate itself from the big boxes and others selling high-end consumer electronics. So Miroglio Architecture + Design (Oakland, Calif.) composed the store along the lines of a jewelry store or museum space, focusing on the industrial design of the merchandise.

The transparent storefront is simply an extension of the interior. As with the rest of the store, the materials are stainless steel, glass, aluminum, maple and marble. A 3-D sign/logo is integrated into the storefront composition.

The interior focus is on the glass pods, vitrines that feature flexible display shelves projecting from clear acrylic poles which themselves extend out of a glowing resin base, all within a 10 foot-tall glass enclosure. (The vitrines have power supplies and data/communications cables.)

CLIENT Futuretronics, Houston – Josh Levy, ceo; Mike Glazer, store development

DESIGN Miroglio Architecture + Design, Oakland, Calif. – Joel Miroglio, principal/design; Patrick Ahearn, associate

GENERAL CONTRACTOR Andrew Maxx Construction, Westerville, Ohio

SUPPLIERS USG, Chicago (ceiling); Móz Designs, Oakland, Calif. (fixtures); Atlas Carpet, City of Commerce, Calif. (flooring); Formica, San Francisco (laminates); A Better Image Sign Co., Castro Valley, Calif. (signage)

PHOTOGRAPHY Joel Gardner Photography, Oakland, Calif.

Mikasa
Woodfield Mall, Schaumburg, Ill.
JGA Inc., Southfield, Mich.

Mikasa wanted a store format that recognized its multi-lifestyle and broad category offering by appealing to a wide variety of customers and segmented around style and design themes to appeal to that variety of attitudes.

The store creates a street of shops, inviting browsers to enjoy the everyday relevance of a tabletop and gift-ware store. The zoned departments showcase the breadth and depth of the line.

The prototype communicates Mikasa's strength as a creative design house through the use of images both dramatic and artistic. Large slab-like fixturing components integrate with internally illuminated blocks and light, open towers, creating lifestyle statements that reinforce both the collection and mix-and-match characteristics of the product while also providing an opportunity for spacious openness and traffic flow.

The window fixturing provides the necessary capacity and depth, but also allows for open, defined areas to highlight individual products.

CLIENT Mikasa, Secaucus, N.J. – Ken Mesnik, executive vp; Jim Linsalata, vp, merchandising; Joe Schkufza, director, store planning; Diane Perry, director, visual presentation

DESIGN JGA Inc., Southfield, Mich. – Ken Nisch, chairman; Kathi McWilliams, creative director; Mike McCahill, project manager

GENERAL CONTRACTOR Sajo, Montreal

OUTSIDE DESIGN CONSULTANT Gary Steffy, Ann Arbor, Mich. (lighting design)

SUPPLIERS Erco, Edison, N.J., Lightolier, Fall River, Mass., Halo/Cooper Industries, Peachtree City, Ga. (lighting); Buell, Dallas (floors); Waterworks, Birmingham, Mich. (wall tile); Builders Furniture Ltd., Winnipeg, Man. (fixtures); Matrix Fixtures Inc., Hastings on Hudson, N.Y. (window pole system); Greneker, Los Angeles (storefront columns); Décor Group, Clawson, Mich. (signage/graphics); Wilsonart, Temple, Texas, Pionite, Auburn, Me. (laminates); VenTec, Chicago (wood); Benjamin Moore, Montvale, N.J. (paint)

PHOTOGRAPHY Laszlo Regos Photography, Berkley, Mich.

Coach
Shibuya District, Tokyo
Michael Neumann Architecture, New York

Tokyo's Shibuya district is the busiest, trendiest shopping area in Japan, and so Coach's store design needed to address several key issues: to respond to its lively retail context with a fresh take on the company's prototypical American image; to attract fast-moving passersby into the store and up to the second level; and to develop furnishings to reflect the upbeat tastes of the young consumer.

The façade is conceived as a lit, 3-D billboard, clad in etched glass. A large rectangular volume wrapped in American walnut projects out and suspends above the sidewalk. A window reveals a glimpse of the second-floor space and product.

On the front façade, a double-height display/entry window opens a view into the multi-level interior.

Inside, the double-height space contains a sweeping open stair of floating travertine treads leading toward the interior. The strong presence of the walnut display box drives customers upstairs to explore. Inside the box, travertine flooring wraps up the wall to provide a rich display surface for cantilevered shelves and floating wall cabinets.

CLIENT Coach Store Design and Visual Merchandising, New York – Reed Krakoff, president, executive creative director; Michael Fernbacher, divisional vp, store design worldwide; Karin Cole, divisional vp, visual merchandising creative worldwide; Peter White, senior manager, international store design; Joy Bruder, director, visual merchandising international and wholesale; Julie McGinnis, director, design services; John Gunter, director, visual merchandising, Japan; Chris Amplo, director, store operations, Japan; Kyoko Hasagawa, manager, visual merchandising international; Tsugio Kurosawa, project manager, Coach Japan Inc.

DESIGN Michael Neumann Architecture, New York – Michael Neumann, principal; Jairo Camelo, project manager; Jeff Rudy, Talin Rudy, senior designers; Mike Raja, Jason DePierre, Tracy Look Hong, project team

GENERAL CONTRACTOR Shimizu Corp., Tokyo

OUTSIDE DESIGN CONSULTANT Worktecht, Tokyo (lighting design)

SUPPLIER Soars Space Produce, Tokyo (fixtures)

PHOTOGRAPHY Nacasa & Partners Inc., Tokyo

Nebraska Furniture Mart
Kansas City, Kan.
Design Forum, Dayton, Ohio

The original Nebraska Furniture Mart is 77 acres and a campus of buildings. The retailer wanted its new 712,000-square-foot Kansas City store to be all under one roof.

But it had to be manageable and shoppable, while still creating an exciting environment for cross-selling. Finally, the mandate for Design Forum (Dayton, Ohio) was to establish NFM as an expert on style and decor trends.

The glass-fronted main entrance opens into an impressive 65-foot rotunda, providing an immediate sense of size while also allowing for selection of merchandise areas.

Three two-story "dream houses" are the core of the space. Each focuses on one room of the house, featuring vignettes that showcase furniture styles, colors and trends while incorporating merchandise from multiple product categories. Dream houses also provide wayfinding and circulation. Each house guides shoppers to the furniture department corresponding to that designated room using a fashion color to define the given department.

CLIENT Nebraska Furniture Mart, Omaha, Neb. – Jeff Lind, Kansas City store director; Michelle Evers, project director

DESIGN Design Forum, Dayton, Ohio – Lee Carpenter, chairman/ceo; Bruce Dybvad, president; Scott Smith, senior vp, design and planning; Don Rethman, senior vp, architecture; Diane Borton, senior account manager; Brady Harding, vp, architecture; Dan Hauser, vp, procurement; Heidi Miller, director, graphic production; Bridget Serena, senior store planner; Andy Fritts, senior environmental designer; Mike Vine, graphic designer; Jason Walker, resource specialist; Missy Donahoe, store planner

GENERAL CONTRACTOR Turner Construction, Kansas City, Mo.

SUPPLIERS Art Guild, Thorofare, N.J., Architectural Arts, Des Moines, Iowa, Module 21, Dayton, Ohio, Store Contract Management, Richmond Hill, Ont., Lozier Store Fixture, Omaha, Neb., Winntech, Kansas City, Mo. (fixtures); Gammapar, Forest, Va., Caesar Ceramics, Swindon, U.K., Dal-Tile, Dallas, Fritz Tile, Mesquite, Texas, Mannington, Calhoun, Ga. (flooring); Design Fabrications, Madison Heights, Mich., Dimensional Innovations, Overland Park, Kan., Heartland Scenic and Costume, Omaha, Neb., LSI, North Canton, Ohio (signage/graphics); Wilsonart, Temple, Texas (laminates); Benjamin Moore, Montvale, N.J., Sherwin-Williams, Cleveland (paint)

PHOTOGRAPHY Jamie Padgett, Padgett & Co., Chicago

Gallery Café
Vancouver Art Gallery, Vancouver, B.C.
Box Interior Design Inc., Vancouver, B.C.

Gallery Café in the prestigious Vancouver Art Gallery was a counter-service facility. But it wanted to create a new, more modern and inviting environment with a high degree of sophistication. It was to be a space that functioned as a café during the day and as an after-hours event space.

The café is situated as a second floor podium, floating away from the walls of its historic backdrop. The key for Box Interior Design (Vancouver, B.C.) was to use the historicism as a foil for the contemporary intervention. On the two walls where this occurs, the banquettes are kept low and drapery on the stairwell side is used to define the room. Custom lighting at the banquette level helps create a new intimacy.

To create drama, a strong punch of color was needed. The existing white ceiling was painted a vibrant burnt orange, further reinforced by the area carpeting and custom banquette lights.

CLIENT Murray Jamieson, Vancouver, B.C.

DESIGN Box Interior Design Inc., Vancouver, B.C. – H. Jay Brooks, Cynthia Penner, principals

GENERAL CONTRACTOR Heron Construction & Millwork Ltd., Richmond, B.C.

SUPPLIERS Maharam, New York, Designtex, New York (fabrics); Durkan through M.R. Evans Trading, Vancouver, B.C. (flooring); Inform Interiors, Vancouver, B.C. (furniture); Light the Store, Vancouver, B.C. (lighting); Arborite through P.S. White, Vancouver, B.C. (laminates)

PHOTOGRAPHY Larry Goldstein Photography, Vancouver, B.C.

Restaurant Soto
Laval, Que.

GHA Shoppingscapes, Montreal

Soto is a well-known sushi restaurant chain in several Montreal locations. Its dining rooms are known for inventive sushi combinations and presentations.

This branch is located within a new lifestyle outdoor center outside of central Montreal and is the first to bring an urban dining experience to the suburbs.

The design takes advantage of the spaciousness of a big-box base building to express open and pure serenity. It evokes an appreciation of nature in its use of space, light, highly textured materials and tailored furniture and fittings.

The design is presented in stages: the approach, at a slick glass exterior façade; the circulation zones differentiated by custom furniture elements; the varying ceiling treatments; the changing textures; and a subtly crafted palette of color.

The sophistication is without intimidation and achieves a luxe look on a tight budget. Finally, it reflects a unique Japanese approach to design: a transcendental amalgamation of tastefulness, elegance and timelessness. Design can be as nourishing a life force as the food itself.

CLIENT Restaurant Soto, Montreal – Kourosh Salas, president

DESIGN GHA Shoppingscapes, Montreal – Denis Gervais, president; Joni Vallon, senior designer; Isabelle Noreau, designer; Julie Bourdeau, junior designer

ARCHITECTS Regis Cote & Associates, Montreal (exterior); Didier Gillon, Montreal (interior)

SUPPLIERS Designtex, Montreal, Avant-Garde, Montreal (fabrics and wallcoverings); Milliken Carpet, Toronto (flooring); Mikade, Montreal (furniture); Union Lighting, Montreal (lighting); Nevamar distributed by McFaddens-Hardwood & Hardware, Montreal (laminates)

PHOTOGRAPHY Yves Lefebvre, Montreal

Liquor Control Board of Ontario
Summerhill Flagship Store, Toronto
Fiorino Design Inc., Toronto

The North Toronto Station at Yonge and Summerhill streets was built in 1916 to be the city's railway hub, but began declining after the opening of Union Station in 1927.

In February 2003, the protected historic site opened as the Liquor Control Board of Ontario's new flagship store, the largest liquor store in Canada and LCBO's most complex store development project to date.

The mission of the interior design firm, Fiorino Design (Toronto), was to analyze the space and plan the interior layout for a seamless flow between the new and existing building elements. Also, to be sensitive to design and innovative detailing, honoring the restored elements of the 88-year-old building.

The 21,000-square-foot store provides the setting for more than 5000 brands, requiring a layout and signage package that identifies the departments and provides wayfinding throughout. The soaring volume of the Great Hall entrance has been substantially restored (in marked contrast to the false ceiling that had cut the 38-foot-high space in half). New materials have been introduced, some sensitive to the historic heritage and some that subtly create a slight frisson of contrast, including terrazo flooring with 50 percent recycled bottle glass.

CLIENT Liquor Control Board of Ontario, Toronto – Jackie Bonic, vp, store development and real estate; Nancy Cardinal, vp, marketing communications

DESIGN Fiorino Design Inc., Toronto – Nella Fiorino, principal; Vilija Gacionis, Amor Jalandoon, Vasco Pires, Mike Wilson, designers/CAD technicians

GENERAL CONTRACTOR Eastern Construction, Toronto

ARCHITECT Goldsmith Borgal & Co. Ltd., Toronto

OUTSIDE DESIGN CONSULTANT Lightbrigade, Toronto (lighting design)

SUPPLIERS Heather Cooper Ltd., Toronto (graphics); Entertainment Technology, Toronto (audio/visual); CCI Woodword, Mississauga, Ont., VIC Store Fixtures, Mississauga, Ont., Wallwood Construction Ltd., Richmond Hill, Ont. (fixtures); Nougart Inc., Toronto, Olympia Tile Co., Toronto, Stone Tile Intl., Toronto, Sullivan Source Inc., Toronto, York Marble, Toronto (flooring); Barbican Architectural Products, Ft. Erie, Ont., Lightolier, Etobicoke, Ont. (lighting); Arborite, Paris, Ont., Formica Canada, Etobicoke, Ont., Nevamar, Mississauga, Ont., Octopus Products, Toronto, Wilsonart Canada, Mississauga, Ont. (laminates and solid surfaces); PCL Graphics, Toronto (inside graphics); Gould Signs Corp., London, Ont. (outside signage); Benjamin Moore & Co., Toronto, Para Paints, Brampton, Ont., Tiger Drylac, Guelph, Ont., Sherwin-Williams, Mississauga, Ont. (paint and wallcoverings)

PHOTOGRAPHY David Whittaker, Toronto

party zone

track 2

COOLERS

Mega
Cuernavaca, Mexico
Pavlik Design Team, Ft. Lauderdale, Fla.

"Perceived by the customer as fresher and better quality than the competitors." That's the goal of most supermarkets, but for a discounter in Mexico it was a considerable design challenge for Pavlik Design Team.

The solutions included a very open store utilizing the space between the merchandise and the ceiling for graphic communication. That bright and exciting graphics package communicates freshness and quality while helping the shopper through the store.

Wide, clearly defined aisles allow for merchandise exposure on both sides as well as merchandise displays in the middle. Featured endcap departments create attention and orient shoppers. Bright colors in the perimeter help the definition of spaces.

Low gondolas allow for better understanding of the space anywhere in the store. High, efficient lighting maintains the store's brightness and expresses freshness. And the circular flooring pattern defines each area and creates logical, interesting traffic flows.

CLIENT Tiendas Comercial Mexicana Mega, Cuernevaca, Mexico – Santiago Garcia, general director; Lamberto Vallejo, director, operations; Javier Cantu, director, projects; Javier Moran, sub-director, operations; Santiago Echeveste, director, services; Eloy Velasco, director, new projects

DESIGN The Pavlik Design Team, Ft. Lauderdale, Fla. – Ron Pavlik, president/ceo; Luis Martin, vp; Luis Valladares, director, design; Placido Herrera, design administrative director; Christy Morales, project designer; Javier Calle, project manager; Ximena Navarrete, graphic designer; Amy Ann S. Ehmcke, lighting designer

ARCHITECT Darq, S.C., Col Moderna, Mexico

SUPPLIERS JM Romo, Aguascalientes, Mexico (fixtures); Formacryl de Mexico SA, Barrio Santiaguito Tultitl, Edo. de Mexico (graphics); Semad, Tultitilan, Edo. de Mexico (furniture and woodwork); Tyler Refrigeration Corp., Col. Anahuac, Mexico (cooler manufacturer); Laminart, Elk Grove Village, Ill., Wilsonart, Miami (laminates); Grupo Industrial Domus, Mexico City (furniture); DuPont, Mexico City (special finish)

PHOTOGRAPHY Dana Hoff, Lake Park, Fla.

Seven
Toronto
Il By IV Design Associates Inc., Toronto

Seven wanted to be Toronto's sexy house and R&B hot dance destination on weekends, yet support a week-day corporate lunch crowd.

The owner, Dynamic Hospitality & Entertainment Group (Toronto), already owned the office building. But it was a somewhat utilitarian space, so a compelling street presence and entry experience was also called for.

Il By IV Design (Toronto) created a single large open lounge area on the main floor centered around a huge, hollow, square bar. The lounge is ringed with 4-foot-tall, internally lit column-like drink tables circled with metal footrails.

The lounge leads to a dazzling dance floor, over-looked by a second lounge on the mezzanine, where pure white, low-profile furnishings repeat the hollow, square layout of the first floor.

The name of the place, referring to the deadly sins, provides the core interior theme. References are sand-blasted in mirror surfaces above the lounge ban-quettes and upstairs behind the 30-foot, internally lit bar. The backlit mirror continuously changes colors, matched by downlighting on the bottle display.

CLIENT Dynamic Hospitality & Entertainment Group, Toronto

DESIGN Il By IV Design Associates Inc., Toronto – Dan Menchions, Keith Rushbrook, principals; Tanya Yeung, Andy Verhiel, designers

SUPPLIERS ISA Intl., Toronto (fabrics); Riverfield Renovations, Toronto (flooring); ISA Intl., Toronto, Kiosk, Toronto, Nienkampter, Toronto, Plan B, Toronto (furniture); Nova Classique, Toronto, Lightolier, Toronto, Eurolite, Toronto (lighting); McFaddens, Oakville, Ont. (laminates); Scenery Plastics, Toronto (wallcoverings)

PHOTOGRAPHY David Whittaker, Toronto

Citizens Bank
Belmont, Mass.

Lippincott Mercer, New York

The new branch prototype was designed to support Citizens' brand positioning, bring its brand personality to life and facilitate the bank's reputation for service.

The open, welcoming environment begins at the street. An impactful storefront appearance uses bold graphics with glowing green frames, 3-D merchandising and other techniques customarily employed by more traditionally mainstream retailers.

The ATM vestibule is a comfortable signature environment that combines wall treatments of solid surface and unexpected touches, such as lively music.

The branch interior is light, bright, clean and crisp. The palette consists of a signature light green paint, maple wood veneer and flooring and warm patterned carpet and furniture. Illuminated "hello" pylons are positioned in the front and back entrances, featuring LCD screens broadcasting the bank's special offers.

Integral to the space are large-scale interior "billboards" that are updated twice a year. The overscaled imagery and single word graphics ("grow") speak the Citizens' voice.

CLIENT Citizens Financial Group, Providence, R.I. – Linda Arel, Charles Carpenter, Gerry Curtin, Theresa McLaughlin, Sheryl Meusert, Claire Smith

DESIGN Lippincott Mercer, New York – Ken Roberts, ceo; Connie Birdsall, creative director; Peter Dixon, senior partner; Randall Stone, partner; Fabian Diaz, Ryan Kovalak, Julia McGreevy, Andres Nicholls, Alexander Reid

GENERAL CONTRACTOR Shawmut Design & Construction, Boston

ARCHITECT Primary Group, Boston

SUPPLIERS Muzak, Charlotte, N.C., Impart, Seattle (audio/video); Armstrong, Lancaster, Pa. (ceiling); Brayton Intl., High Point, N.C., Kimball, Jasper, Ind., Steelcase, Grand Rapids, Mich. (fabrics, furniture); Michael Pera Inc., Manchester, N.H. (millwork); Masland, New York (flooring); Millennium Group, Hempstead, N.Y. (graphics, props/decoratives); Flos Inc., Huntington Station, N.Y., Indy Lighting, Fisher, Ind., LSI Lightron, Cincinnati (lighting); Formica, Cincinnati, Wilsonart, Temple, Texas (laminates); Philadelphia Sign Co., Palmyra, N.J. (signage); Enterprises Inc., Boston (glass film)

PHOGOGRAPHY Adrian Wilson, New York

Awards of Merit Winners

Sears Grand
Jordan Landing Plaza, West Jordan, Utah
The Pavlik Design Team, Fort Lauderdale, Fla.

The new Sears Grand prototype in West Jordan, Utah, is a one-level standalone store designed to be "a unique Sears experience" – a wide product and brand assortment in a value-oriented, contemporary environment intended to diffentiate Sears from its competitors.

As well as from itself. This store was not to be confused with a Sears department store. This, said the retailer, is mass-merchandising with a new customer-focused attitude. Outside and in.

Three white icon slabs on the outside provide a clean, modern storefront anchoring an all-blue and glass structure. According to designers from The Pavlik Design Team, exposed cross bracing in the glass vestibule combine an industrial gesture for "value" with the "stylish" slab walls of the storefront.

The elongated shape of thew building provides for maximized storefront exposure, while the shallow footprint allows the back of the store to remain approachable.

Three aisle systems combine with a main boulevard to connect the three worlds of Home Fashions, Apparel and Home Improvement. Centralized checkouts at the front of the store bridge the two main entrances and seasonal products.

Central pads are anchored by three pavilions providing architectural volume, hierarchy and layering of merchandise stories, as well as fitting rooms and shoe stock. Architectural proscenium frames span from pad to pad, bringing the volume of space to human scale. Lifestyle messages along the boulevard and merchandised slab walls on the pads provide an architectural rhythm and add excitement to the shopping experience.

CLIENT Sears Roebuck & Co., Hoffman Estates, Ill. – Fred Rosenberg, cp, facilities, planning and construction; David Rich, vp, store planning; Russell Arnold, vp, construction; Rosemary Kastrava, vp, visual merchandising and in-store marketing; Jerry Post, senior vp, off-the-mall strategy; Teresa Byrd, vp/gmm, off-the-mall stores

DESIGN The Pavlik Design Team, Fort Lauderdale, Fla. – Ron Pavlik, president, ceo; Armando Castillo, director of projects; Sherif Ayad, creative director; Placido Herrera, design administrative director; Amy Neumann, project planner; Diana Santiago, project manager; Wendy Wright, project designer; Tiera Lindsey, assistant project designer; Amy Ann S. Ehmcke, lighting designer; Ximena Navarrete, Jennifer Veltre, graphic designers

ARCHITECT S.A. Miro Inc., Denver

SUPPLIERS Lozier, Omaha, Neb., Cap & Assoc., Columbus, Ohio, Harbor Industries, Grand Haven, Mich., Pan-Oston, Glasgow, Ky., Borroughs, Kalamazoo, Mich., Ready Metal Mfg., Chicago, Amstore, Muskegon, Mich. (fixtures); Bernstein, Port Washington, N.Y., Trimco, Brooklyn, ALU, New York (forms and decoratives); Consolidated Electrical Distributors, Naperville, Ill. (lighting); Mohawk, Kennesaw, Ga., Armstrong, Lancaster, Pa., Centiva, Florence, Ala. (flooring); MDC, Chicago (wallcoverings); GFX Intl., Grayslake, Ill. (signage and graphics); Shelby Williams, Chicago (furniture); Wilsonart, Temple, Texas (laminate)

PHOTOGRAPHY Dan Sjostrom, Hoffman Estates, Ill.

John L. Morris, Worldwide Sportsman
Destin, Fla.

Bass Pro Shops Inc. Architects, Springfield, Mo.

On the surface, the objective of this project was to design a specialty retail shop, with departments for hunting, fishing, camping, gifts, apparel, sunglasses, boating, marine and boat service.

But the underlying objective, and the more challenging goal, was to create an engaging and immersive experience geared towards the primary target markets of local outdoor enthusiasts and the booming tourist trade. And yet even more underlying was reflecting the area's coastal environment and the region's rich, enduring cultural heritage.

Planning solutions ranged from the simple boathouse shape to the two-level interior. From the nautical character of the steel frame trusses to the petroglyphs carved into the oceanic finish of the floors, every component of the project was utilized to address the various design and styling issues.

Many of the special features and finishes were designed in collaboration with dedicated blacksmiths, artisans and fabricators – the pelican copper lanterns, the metalworked gates adorned with offshore fishing forms, the original artwork on the walls, the custom-built chandeliers, the taxidermy mounts modeled to reflect the movement of local fish.

The key to the success of this project was the close affiliation of its designers and merchants. Involving both from beginning to end in a non-linear development process produced an integrated design beyond the vision of any one group. Much like the boat-shaped checkouts, the design is a melding of aesthetics and utility.

CLIENT Bass Pro Shops Inc., Springfield, Mo. – Tom Jowett, vp, design and development; Tom Gammon, director of construction; Mark Tuttle, director of architecture; Lenny Clark, senior technical designer; Glennon Scheid, interior project manager; Jim Gallagher, project manager; Monica Matthias, interior project manager, fixtures and signage; Rick Collins, taxidermy; Russ Halley, project interior color, material, finish selections; Bruce Teter, retail planning director

GENERAL CONTRACTOR Centex Rooney, Destin, Fla.

ARCHITECT Butler Rosenbury & Partners, Springfield, Mo.

OUTSIDE DESIGN CONSULTANTS Spaid Associates, Springfield, Mo. (landscape architect); Larson Binkley Inc., Kansas City, Kan. (MEP engineers)

SUPPLIERS Lozier, Omaha, Neb., Wood Systems, Tulsa, Okla. (fixtures); Garage Graphics, Springfield, Mo. (graphics); Bass Pro Fabrication Shop, Nixa, Mo., Rocky Creek Ltd., Stephensville, Texas, Classic Displays, Grand Rapids, Mich., White Oak Displays, Manheim, Pa. (decoratives and props)

PHOTOGRAPHY Douglas Hill, Snellville, Ga.

Express Design Studio
Mall of America, Bloomington, Minn.
Limited Store Design & Construction, Columbus, Ohio

Limited Brands wanted to celebrate the Express fashion brand and a team of designers "dedicated to the relentless pursuit of perfection for the brand. These designers are the unsung heroes behind Express."

To celebrate these heroes, Limited Brands created the Express Design Studio, a shop concept located near the front door of the Express store. The introduction begins at the storefront, with a mural of the team in the window, using red acrylic panels and sexy mannequins featuring the team's fashion creations.

As customers enter the store, designers' faces greet them from back-lit acrylic panels set on top of the shelves. Designers' names and background accompany their photographs. The atelier photos seen in adjacent cabinets reflect the designers' day-to-day lives. Another cabinet contains a Design Studio quote that describes the studio and its mission statement.

New fixtures and navigation system help support the Design Studio mission. A paired Boris fixture is a clean and simple design with high capacity and display opportunities. There are three pull-out drawers on one side and a hanging bar on the other.

The display wall fixture is a high-fashion piece with a clear plexiglass "wall" and UV white- and red-finished display base. A new entry table is also designed for different store configurations along with the award-winning, red Express "O" fixture.

The new navigation system includes the fit menu, which names the styles, and the shelf talkers, which allow the customer to locate different styles and sizes.

CLIENT Limited Brands, Express Design Studio, Mall of America, Bloomington, Minn.
DESIGN Limited Store Design & Construction, Columbus, Ohio – Michael Lee, design manager; Roger Sherwood, design consultant
PHOTOGRAPHY Benny Chan, Santa Monica, Calif.

I.N.C. Missy Shop
Macy's Herald Square, New York
Federated Merchandising Group, New York

I.N.C. International Concept, launched in 1991 as a casual jeans and T-shirt line in Missy sportswear, has become a nationally recognized private-label brand offering a full collection of updated contemporary clothing.

But Federated felt it needed to freshen the I.N.C. in-store environment, using Macy's flagship as the testing ground. It also expanded the I.N.C. shop to 1400 square feet.

The modern, pared-down design of the shop is a study in contrast between light and dark. T-stands use a combination of frosted Plexiglas and stainless steel. Campaign images float in large Plexi frames resting on dark wooden shelves. A trend area is carved down the center of the shop to feature the most fashion-forward merchandise. Rows of pin spotlights illuminate the area like a runway.

Three-mannequin platforms, up-lit from the base, run down the aisle, framed by curving racks and feature tables. The mannequins, designed to capture the international concept of the brand, are a mix of African, Asian, Caucasian and Latin ethnicities.

Sweeping panels behind the cashwraps at the rear of the shop were fabricated of gouged thalweg, adding an interesting texture to the otherwise smooth surfaces. Five lightboxes feature images from the current ad campaign.

CLIENT Federated Department Stores, Cincinnati

DESIGN Federated Merchandising Group Visual & Shop Design Team, New York – Joe Feczko, evp, marketing; Ron Bausman, vp, visual and shop development; Young de Charette, design director; Brian Ford, project director; Kevin McKenna, visual manager; Macy's Herald Square visual team

GENERAL CONTRACTOR Creative Corp., New York – Jean Claude Garcia

SUPPLIERS JP Metal, Montreal (fixtures); Store Lighting Systems, New York (lighting); Rootstein, New York, Goldsmith, Long Island City, N.Y. (mannequins); Color Edge Visual, New York, Coe Displays, Long Island City, N.Y. (signage); Architectural Systems, New York (wallcoverings)

PHOTOGRAPHY Ricky Zehavi, Brooklyn

Harrods White Hall
London
Callison Architecture Inc., Seattle

Harrods, the London department store icon, recognized that the cosmetics retailing trend is changing. But it also knew it didn't want to tinker with its White Hall, a room known for architectural grandeur and splendor.

Specifically, the trend toward customized products and services had rendered the old model – subtle indirect lighting, island counters, product under glass – obsolete.

In the new design, the Hall has a strong central aisle lined with special promotion sites and a variety of display options for customers' experimentation. Layout and fixtures are designed to invite customers into each brand zone to interact with "advisors." Testers, seating, mirrors and lamps were all specially designed to complement the overall room design.

All 26 beauty brands in the room were given a uniform kit of parts by which to define their product displays: casework, standardized testers, hand-held mirrors, counter stools and designated promotional areas.

Replacing the old dark, indirect lighting is brightness, warmth, glow and color-correctness. Shelves are back-lit and casework is under-lit. The testers and casework all have a curved, under-lit skirting that illuminates the circulation areas. At the center of it all, a lustrous chandelier of hand-blown, clear crystal and white flowers replaces a smaller light fixture that once hung in the middle of the room.

CLIENT Harrods White Hall, London – John England, Peter Hall, Mervyn Ashdown, project directors, Davies Shopfitters

DESIGN Callison Architecture Inc., Seattle – M.J. Munsell, principal in charge; Dawn Clark, principal, client manager; Elizabeth Buxton, design lead; Joel Riehl, project architect; Joe Webber, Dave Brown, Som Khouvong, Christian Jochman, architectural staff; Erin Krohn, Barry Shuman, designers

SUPPLIERS Ozone Glass, Brighton, U.K. (special glass); A. Bernacca & Co., Carrara, Italy (marble); B. Sweden, Bath, U.K. (lighting); Barretts Glass & Window Centre Ltd., Dorchester, U.K. (glass tops)

PHOTOGRAPHY David Perks, Wallington, Surrey, U.K.

Nordstrom Designers Group
Fashion Show Mall, Las Vegas
Callison Architecture Inc., Seattle

Aiming specifically at the Las Vegas market, Nordstrom wanted to develop distinctive environments for the various attitudes within the fashion world for its store in Fashion Show Mall: the couture evening-wear level; the collectors upscale, classic-designer level; and "via C" for trendy, rising-star designers.

Working with Callison, the retailer developed tiered specialty-store environments for each designer department, reinforcing the merchandise mix and sales approach within each.

"Via C," the new concept shop for rising-star designers, is an eclectic space created to appeal to the well-traveled fashionista. Designers stayed authentic to that customer profile all the way through the dressing room's rich mix of materials, antiques and Asian objets d'art.

CLIENT Nordstrom Inc., Seattle – Nancy Webber, interiors and concept design lead; Paige Boggs, design planner, women's designer apparel; Steve Cockburn, casework coordinator, women's designer apparel; Susan Morton, interiors and concept design manager

DESIGN Callison Architecture Inc., Seattle – M.J. Munsell, principal in charge; Curtis Hughes, Ron Singler, Christian Jochman, Dave Brown, Anneka O'Connell, Ching Chung, designers

SUPPLIERS J.F. Chen Antiques, Los Angeles (furnishings); Heartwood, Seattle, Universal Showcase, Woodbridge, Ont. (fixtures); Syracuse Flooring, E. Syracuse, N.Y., Architectural Systems, New York (flooring); Charles Loomis Inc., Kirkland, Wash. (lighting); Carolyn Ray, Yonkers, N.Y. (wallcovering); Walton Signage, San Antonio, Texas (signage)

PHOTOGRAPHY Chris Eden, Seattle

Orly
Carrefour Laval Shopping Center, Laval, Que.
DSD Groupe Design, Montreal

Orly selected an appropriate diamond shaped corner location for its jewelry and watch store in the newly expanded Carrefour Laval Shopping Center.

Focusing on the power of this location, designers used a fan-like layout to establish the store's rhythm. One of the main objectives was to create a dynamic environment by combining stainless steel with a sense of transparency to emulate the jewelry.

The focal point is the angled corner column with a display window, supporting an art deco-style luminous bulkhead, crowned with a corner clock.

Radiating lines of the terrazzo floor pattern branch off this focal element and accentuate the diamond-shaped entrance. Each floor line coincides with individual counter units, while lighting and ceiling suspension elements follow the floor pattern.

The remaining materials were limited to clear and sandblasted glass and dark natural wood. Recessed deep blue neon tubing behind the sandblasted glass back wall and over the floating ceilings provides a subtle hue and accent.

CLIENT Orly , Montreal

DESIGN DSD Groupe Design, Montreal – Dimitri Smolens, senior designer, concept creator; Pascal Marthet, artistic director; Hervé Legrand, technical designer; Katie Jones, assistant designer

GENERAL CONTRACTOR Avicor Construction, Montreal

OUTSIDE DESIGN CONSULTANT Vladimir Subert, Sutton, Que. (illustrator)

SUPPLIERS Céramique Champlain, Montreal (flooring); Nemus, Montreal (furniture); Lumitech, Montreal (lighting); Media-Modul, Montreal (signage)

PHOTOGRAPHY Christian Fleury, Montreal

Palm Store Century City
Los Angeles
B&N Industries, Burlingame, Calif.

Designers of the brick-and-mortar store for Palm Handhelds felt it was important that customers be able to interact with the small products. Also, the palm-sized products couldn't get lost in the overall design of the space.

B&N Industries (Burlingame, Calif.) designers used floor-to-ceiling café tables to display the handheld products and encourage interaction among customers. All wiring to power the products and lighting is concealed inside the freestanding table units.

Along one side of the store, product collections and accessories are spotlighted in a series of backlit cubbies and suspended casework installed along the wall. On the opposite wall, giant closets house backstock behind sliding doors which are disguised by large graphics of Palm products.

Lighting, music and a clean design further play up the lounge-like atmosphere, while the overall white store palette is punched up with orange accents, the company's signature color.

Following the interior's clean design cues, the storefront is minimally framed in glass, affording clear views inside.

CLIENT Palm Inc., Milpitas, Calif.

DESIGN B&N Industries, Burlingame, Calif. – Kevin McPhee, image director; Pirkko Lucchesi, project manager

GENERAL CONTRACTOR Vertical Retail Solutions, Andover, Conn.

ARCHITECT Askew Nixon Ferguson Architects, Memphis, Tenn.

SUPPLIERS DMX Music, Los Angeles (audio/video); Moss Inc., Belfast, Maine (fabrics); B&N Industries, Burlingame, Calif. (fixturing); Cherner Chair Co., Westport, Conn. (furniture); JP Digital, Mountain View, Calif. (graphics)

PHOTOGRAPHY Scott Van Dyke, Palm Springs, Calif.

Reebok Women's Concept Store
New York

Kramer Design Group, New York

Aiming to provide women with a store offering the latest in athletic gear as well as delivering educational and health information to shoppers, Reebok designed its Concept Store as a living magazine. "Editorial walls," comprised of glass and steel, are positioned throughout the store, highlighting the latest trends and seasonal merchandise, as well as stories or informational bits. For example, a wall on breast cancer may include health information as well as the latest pink sports bras.

The goal to inform shoppers is also achieved through a ticker tape message board that carries illuminated health messages aimed at women. The board runs along the shoe bar, where glass balls hold athletic shoes upside down so that shoppers can see the technology of the shoe, while its pair sits upright on top of it.

Adding movement throughout the store are random colored slats on the walls and smooth, curving stainless-steel fixtures. On the floor, pebbles embedded in clear resin create a floating effect.

At the giraffe wood cashwrap, customers can sit on bar stools and read an electronic bulletin board or interact with staff.

CLIENT Reebok Intl. Ltd., Canton, Mass. – Paul Fireman, president; Larry Gore, senior vp, global retail; Anderson McNeill, vp of full price; Janet Ries, director, design services; Peter Quagge, design services manager; Jody Remaklus, senior graphic design manager; Doug Noonan, vp, corporate real estate and facilities; Stephen Becker, global project manager

DESIGN Kramer Design Group, New York – Robin Kramer, president and creative director; Philip Rosenzweig, creative director; Merton Wu, project designer; Laura Boyd, Victor Herrera, designers

GENERAL CONTRACTOR Structuretone, New York

ARCHITECT BKA Associates, Brockton, Mass.

OUTSIDE DESIGN CONSULTANT Schweppe Lighting Design Inc., Concord, Mass.

SUPPLIERS Sound System, Northboro, Mass. (audio); James Wickstead Design Associates, Cedar Knoll, N.J. (video, vacuum fluorescent display); Environments, Minnetonka, Minn. (fixturing); Robin Reigi, New York (flooring); B&B Italia, New York (furniture); Sign Design Inc., Brockton, Mass. (graphics); Central Electrical Specialty Corp., Brockton, Mass. (lighting); Goldsmith, Long Island City, N.Y. (mannequins); Lifestyle Forms and Display Co. Inc., New York (forms); Alto Sign, Philadelphia (signage)

PHOTOGRAPHY James Lattanzio, Montclair, N.J.

Samuel Getz Jewelers
Coral Gables, Fla.

Echeverria Design Group, Coral Gables, Fla.

Jewelry has been sold in private salons in Europe for centuries. Samuel Getz, a third-generation U.S. jeweler, decided to transplant that concept to South Florida. The underlying idea was to create a selling environment that helps clients feel completely at ease, as if they were sitting in a friend's home.

To create that setting, Echeverria Design Group (Coral Gables, Fla.) employed exotic woods, leather furniture and a subdued earthtone palette throughout the 2200-square-foot salon, which is subdivided into areas roughly resembling a living room, a dining room and a bar. "The intent is to create a 'soft-sell' environment," says Mario Echeverria, president.

Getz's sumptuous salon is housed in an office building that's part of the stylish Village of Merrick Park mixed-use complex in Coral Gables.

CLIENT Samuel Getz Jewelers, Coral Gables, Fla. – Samuel Getz, owner

DESIGN Echeverria Design Group, Coral Gables, Fla. – Mario Echeverria, president; John Naranjo, senior designer; Chris Cortes, production

GENERAL CONTRACTOR Solutions General Contractors, Miami

OUTSIDE DESIGN CONSULTANTS KLG Engineering, Atlanta; Donnell, Duquense & Albaisa, Miami

SUPPLIERS Brentano Inc., Northbrook, Ill. (curtain); Tuohy Inc., Chatfield, Minn. (leather); Creative Cabinets, Miami (fixturing); New Stone Age Inc., Miami, Vega World Supply, Elizabeth, N.J. (flooring); Arredo, Coral Gables, Fla., Tuohy Inc., Chatfield, Minn., Jeffrey Michaels, Design Center of the Americas, Dania, Fla. (furniture); Sesco Lighting, Ft. Lauderdale, Fla., Florida Architectural Lighting, Ft. Lauderdale, Fla. (lighting); Formica, Cincinnati (laminates); Innovations in Wall-covering, Design Center of the Americas, Dania, Fla. (wallcoverings)

PHOTOGRAPHY Dan Forer, Miami

Timberland
The Ginza, Tokyo
FRCH Design Worldwide, Cincinnati

Timberland's new Ginza flagship in Tokyo, the first store the company has opened outside the domestic market in several years, represents the latest evolution of the brand.

The main entry of the two-level, 2500-square-foot space houses the first of two major water features. This simple stacked-stone and river rock waterfall combines with a media presentation to establish an immediate connection with nature, functioning as a decompression zone so shoppers can leave the high-traffic shopping district behind. It also calls out the Timberland culture.

Once shoppers pass the transition zone, they encounter a long, linear presentation table made of seeded glass. A seeded glass ceiling trellis serves as a focal feature to display seasonal elements like fall leaves or winter ice crystals. These pieces draw shoppers' eyes back to the cashwrap, where a stacked stone wall with a large-scale Roman copper Timberland tree is set against amber glass panel.

Adjacent to the branded cashwrap is the staircase, a Zen-inspired stone garden that marks the entry to the path upstairs. A two-story filament water feature adds a calming and serene element representation of the Japanese lifestyle. The staircase itself is made out of cantilevered, textured concrete, which comes out from the wall, and is lit from the underside for added drama.

CLIENT Timberland, Stratham, N.H. – Bevan Bloemendaal, senior director, global creative services; Carol Yang, senior marketing director, Asia Pacific; Shizuka Aoki, visual merchandising executive, Japan; Celine Teo, visual merchandising manager, Asia Pacific; Osamu Nakayama, retail operation manager, Japan; Naoya Sakamoto, visual merchandiser

DESIGN FRCH Design Worldwide, Cincinnati – Paul Lechleiter, principal-in-charge, chief creative officer; Christian Davies, vp, design strategy, and creative director; Scott Frazier, project director; Mari Miura, interior design; Lori Kolthoff, resource design director

GENERAL CONTRACTOR Okamura Corp., Tokyo

ENGINEER Shinkougei Co. Ltd., Tokyo

SUPPLIERS Shinkougei Co. Ltd., Tokyo (fabric, fixturing, signage, special metal, specialty glass); Board Co. Ltd., Tokyo (bamboo flooring); Okamura Corp., Tokyo (fixturing); LCD Mfg., Kingston, N.Y. (leather); Lighting Management Inc., New City, N.Y. (lighting); One by One Co., Osaka, Japan (perimeter wall system); Albero Co. Ltd., Tokyo (reclaimed wood); Advan, Tokyo (stone); Cultured Stone Corp., Napa, Calif. (stacked stone); Matsushita Electric Industrial Co. Ltd., Osaka, Japan (video system); Atelier Progres, Tokyo (washi paper, stone garden); Water Pearl Co. Ltd., Tokyo (water feature)

PHOTOGRAPHY Masami Fukuda, Tokyo

authentics

International Spy Museum Store
Washington, D.C.

FRCH Design Worldwide, Cincinnati

Visitors to the International Spy Museum in Washington, D.C., are immersed in a series of interactive exhibits that let them adopt a cover, break codes, identify disguised spies and become the subjects of covert surveillance. That emphasis on interactivity carries over into the 5000-square-foot Spy Museum Store, which FRCH Design Worldwide (Cincinnati) created in conjunction with the museum's advisory board and its team of architecture and design firms.

FRCH's mission – which it chose to accept – was "to extend the museum experience into the store, so visitors could interact with the merchandise, satisfy their curiosity and outfit themselves for a personal spy mission," says Steve McGowan, vp/creative director.

The interactive experience continues in the transition area between the museum and the store, where visitors are recorded by a hidden camera. Those images are then displayed on video monitors at the store's entrance. Similarly, visitors to the restaurant adjacent to the store can spy on shoppers through a series of hidden portals.

The store's merchandise is housed in a series of themed shops, including the Spy Library, Spy Disguises, Spy Collectibles and Spy Hollywood.

"The merchandise is offered up in vignettes that mirror the museum's presentation of the tradecraft and history of espionage, as well as popular interpretations of the profession," says Paul Lechleiter, FRCH's principal-in-charge/chief creative officer.

CLIENT International Spy Museum, Washington, D.C. – Milton Maltz, chairman and founder; Mike Devine, cfo; Dennis Barrie, president; Kathy Coakley, vp

DESIGN FRCH Design Worldwide, Cincinnati – Paul Lechleiter, principal-in-charge/chief creative officer; Steve McGowan, vp/creative director; Jay Kratz, design architect; Janet Wernke, project director; Mari Miura, Scott Rink, designers; Aaron Ruef, graphic designer; Jeff Waggoner, graphic design director; Brian Sullivan, construction documentation; Lori Kolthoff, Christie Kratzer, directors, color and materials

GENERAL CONTRACTOR James G. Davis Construction, Washington, D.C.

ARCHITECT SmithGroup, Washington, D.C.

OUTSIDE DESIGN CONSULTANTS Gallagher & Associates, Baltimore (museum design); Mark G. Anderson Consultants, Washington, D.C. (project management); Edwards Technologies Inc., El Segundo, Calif. (audio/visual design); Northern Light Productions, Boston (film and video design); Lighting Management Inc., New City, N.Y. (lighting); J.G. Stanley & Co., New York (retail product consultant)

SUPPLIERS Design Fabricators Inc., a Leggett & Platt Co., Lafayette, Colo. (fixtures/signage); Photo Assist, Bethesda, Md. (photography); Rudy Art Glass Studio, York, Pa. (specialty glass)

PHOTOGRAPHY All images © International Spy Museum, Washington, D.C.

LensCrafters
Tippecanoe Mall, Lafayette, Ind.
Chute Gerdeman, Columbus, Ohio

During the 1990s, the centerpiece of LensCrafters' stores was its in-store laboratory, where customers' eyeglasses were prepared in an hour. But as competitors have weighed in with quick-service eyeglass labs of their own, LensCrafters decided its stores should place more emphasis on selling eyewear as a fashion accessory.

LensCrafters' in-house design team partnered with Chute Gerdeman (Columbus, Ohio) to create a remodeled 4100-square-foot store that balances and integrates the retail space, the eye-exam office and the waiting areas. The underlying goal is to offer additional areas for social interaction, but still reinforce the LensCrafters' brand.

Eyeglass frames are displayed in armoires and glass-topped cases. To let customers see what a given set of frames looks like on them, the store offers countertop image-capture fixtures that allow people to take pictures of themselves. (After taking a shot, customers can put their existing glasses back on to get a clear look at how they look in the new frames.)

Overall, the space features a clean, upscale look, with light and dark wood finishes, stone accents and soft lighting. Large-scale graphics and iconic signage help guide customers through the space. And because research into buyers' behavior found that LensCrafters customers often ask other patrons for their opinions on frames, several common areas are interspersed throughout the space to encourage social interaction.

CLIENT LensCrafters, Mason, Ohio – Bink Zengel, senior design manager, branded environments; Patricia Richie, associate vp, strategy; Cindy Wise, senior project manager, operations; Janet Duke, foresight store strategist; Jay Clements, manager, systems development; Jim Ackner, construction manager

DESIGN Chute Gerdeman, Columbus, Ohio – Denny Gerdeman, principal; Mindi Trank, senior project manager; Tony Oliver, creative director, environments; Eric Daniel, creative director, graphic design; Nicole Vachow, director, visual merchandising; Steven Boreman, Jennifer Linn, graphic designers; Susan Siewny, director, graphic production; Tina Burnham, graphic production coordinator; Carem Costinescu, materials librarian

ARCHITECT WD Partners, Columbus, Ohio

OUTSIDE DESIGN CONSULTANT Schuler & Shook, Minneapolis (lighting)

SUPPLIERS Wolf Gordon Inc., Long Island City, N.Y., Pollack, Beachwood, Ohio, Unika Vaev, Norwood, N.J., Designtex Hospitality, New York, The Bradbury Collection, Hollywood, Calif. (fabrics); Permastellisa, Enfield, Conn. (fixturing); Masland, Saraland, Ala., CDC Contract Flooring, Columbus, Ohio (flooring); Carter Furniture, Salisbury, N.C., Loewenstein, Columbus, Ohio, HBF Furniture, Hickory, N.C., Keilhauer, Toronto; Design Within Reach, San Francisco, Calif. (furniture); Argus Images, Lexington, Ohio, Store Image Programs, Brantford, Ont. (graphics); 100 Watt Network, San Francisco (lighting); Abet Laminati, Englewood, N.J. (laminates); Triangle Sign, Baltimore (signage); Lanark Wallcovering, Hackensack, N.J., American Acrylic Corp., West Babylon, N.Y., Hamilton Parker, Columbus, Ohio (wallcoverings); Armstrong World Industries, Lancaster, Pa. (ceiling); Sherwin Williams, Cleveland, Ohio (paint)

PHOTOGRAPHY Mark Steele, Columbus, Ohio

UltraFemme
Cancun, Mexico
FRCH Design Worldwide, Cincinnati

UltraFemme's 9000-square-foot prototype offers an open-sell environment catering to sophisticated and confident female consumers seeking high-end cosmetics, perfume, watches, fine jewelry and intimate apparel. The store's bold yet simple motif is reflected by the oval columns that dominate the space and reinforce its architectural brand identity.

UltraFemme's cosmetics and fragrance area houses a modular fixture system displaying scents and makeup from such international beauty brands as Chanel, Dior and Lancome. This part of the store also houses a circular cosmetics and fragrance bar, where smoldering, iridescent glass mosaic tiles create a dramatic backdrop for patrons trying the latest scents and makeup. A separate

"Gen Y" zone, targeting younger shoppers, is set off with a dropped ceiling element, several flat-screen monitors and a localized sound system.

The store's lingerie is sold in the Adora boutique, which features such brands as La Perla, Simone Perele, Passionata and Chantelle. Virtually every design element within the shop – including the scalloped carpet and the cashwrap – features sensuous curves.

CLIENT Grupo UltraFemme, Cancun, Mexico – Jose and Elena de Garcia, owners

DESIGN FRCH Worldwide Design, Cincinnati – Paul Lechleiter, principal-in-charge, partner, chief creative officer; Steve McGowan, vp, creative director; Scott Rink, designer; Tracey Williams, graphic design; Lori Kolthoff, resource design

PHOTOGRAPHY Mark A. Steele Photography, Columbus, Ohio

Victoria's Secret
Somerset North, Troy, Mich.
Limited Brands Inc., Columbus, Ohio

Designed to be as striking and dynamic as its lingerie products and the supermodels who wear them, Victoria's Secret's mall prototype store debuted at Somerset North Mall (Troy, Mich.) in July 2003.

Three main openings lead into the 10,000-square-foot store. The Grand Entrance is flanked by two large scaffold fixtures outfitted with realistic mannequins in sexy poses. Windows on either side house a single life-like mannequins, while also permitting views inside.

Focusing on the playful and colorful products, designers from Limited Brands created a store environment that allowed the physical store to recede and let the merchandise stand out. A cosmopolitan palette of cream and black with subtle accents of the retailer's signature pink sets the tone. Black and white graphics and high-gloss black and cream fixtures and finishes further add to the sleek yet sophisticated store environment.

Display cube insets mounted on focal walls display individually lit bra and panty forms, while emphasizing the product categories within each room of the store. Victoria's Secret's new PINK! line, targeting young girls with hip fashions, has a place all its own, featuring a bright and clean palette that is attractive to its youthful shopper, while also tying in with the rest of the store environment.

CLIENT Limited Brands Inc., Columbus, Ohio – Gene Torchia, president; Kathleen Baldwin, Scott Taylor, vps in charge; Polly Sinesi, design manager, Victoria's Secret Store; Shirley Schmitter, director of design, Victoria's Secret Store; Liz Elert, senior vp, visual merchandising; Kathleen Grady, Jason Milburn, purchasing managers; Dick Immenschuh, project manager; Ed Hofmann, director of design, New York; Anne Baxter, specialty finishes

GENERAL CONTRACTOR Commercial Contractors, Holland, Mich.

ARCHITECT McCall Design Group, San Francisco

OUTSIDE DESIGN CONSULTANT Grenald Waldron Associates, Philadelphia

SUPPLIERS PlayNetwork, Redmond, Wash. (audio); Kravet, New York (drapery); Circle Fabric, New York (PINK! shop fabrics); Sajo Inc., Montreal, LT Custom Furnishings, Toronto (fixturing); Innovative Marble & Tile, Hauppauge, N.Y. (flooring); Interior Crafts, Chicago, Galerkin, Gardena, Calif. (furniture); Fuel Digital, New York (graphics); Photobition, New York (PINK! graphics); Capitol Light, Hartford, Conn. (lighting); Lamin-Art, Schaumburg, Ill. (laminates); Patina-V, City of Industry, Calif., Fusion, Broomfield, Colo., Ronis Bros. Lynbrook, N.Y. (mannequins/forms); IDMD Design & Manufacturing, Toronto, Ledan, Mineola, N.Y., Skyframe, New York (props/decoratives); Ruggles Sign, Lexington, Ky. (signage); Maya Romanoff, Chicago, Fashion Wallcoverings, Cleveland (wallcoverings)

PHOTOGRAPHY © Peter Aaron, Esto Photographics Inc., Mamaroneck, N.Y.

Roche-Bobois
Toronto
Figure 3 Network, Toronto

Roche-Bobois, a Paris-based manufacturer of fine residential furniture, chose two adjoining steel-and-brick 1940s office buildings to house its retail flagship in Toronto. The challenge to design firm Figure 3 Network (Toronto): convert the space into a single, distinctive retail environment that supports the reputation and quality of the brand.

Designers answered that brief by merging the two spaces under a two-story atrium that serves as the store's central focus. Surrounding the atrium is a series of smaller galleries housing furniture collections displayed in room vignettes.

Overall, the space utilizes a neutral palette with color accents that allows the merchandise to stand out. Sustainable materials, including bamboo, seagrass and stone flooring, complement the furniture and accessories. To help draw patrons to the second floor, a glass-and-metal staircase topped by a bridge structure was installed.

Outside, much of the building's brick façade was left intact, with new windows and signage added to update its look and feel.

CLIENT Roche-Bobois, Toronto – Laurent Debu, director general

DESIGN Figure 3 Network, Toronto – Christopher Wright, design partner; Kate Verbitskaia, project manger; Steve Tsai, project designer

GENERAL CONTRACTOR Urbacon Ltd., Toronto

ARCHITECT Jeux de Plan, Paris

SUPPLIERS Bay Bloor Radio, Toronto (audio/video); Roche-Bobois, Toronto (fabrics, furniture, props/decoratives); Urbacon Ltd. (fixturing); Crossley, Halifax, Nova Scotia, Silkroad, Toronto, Sullivan Source, Toronto (flooring); Eurolite, Toronto (lighting); Formica, Cincinnati (laminates); WSI Signs, Brampton, Ont. (signage)

PHOTOGRAPHY Richard Johnson, Toronto

Victoria's Secret
Herald Square, New York

Limited Brands Inc., Columbus, Ohio

Victoria's Secret and its parent company, Limited Brands (Columbus, Ohio), used New York's Herald Square flagship to show off the new face of its brand and store design.

The goal was to create a shopping experience representative of the Victoria's Secret lifestyle: sophisticated, sexy, modern, feminine and loaded with attitude. The basic color palette of the store is cream and black, with subtle touches of pink used throughout.

The main floor features three halls with an escalator well in the middle. The first is the "Great Hall," where customers find the most fashion-forward products. Flanking the escalators and wrapped inside the lingerie space is the Beauty store. The third hall is home to a special panty boutique.

The second floor is an array of eight rooms broken out by all the current bra and panty sub-brands.

Perhaps the biggest attention-getter for the store is its mannequins. In the past, Victoria's Secret had used only bust forms. In order to bring the store to life, designers worked with Patina-V to develop realistic mannequins with sexy, provocative poses. In the end,

five different skin tones and faces were created to play back to the specialty retailer's real-life models.

CLIENT Limited Brands Store Design and Construction, Columbus, Ohio – Gene Torchia, president; Scott Taylor, vp; Kathleen Baldwin, vp, design; Polly Miles, senior designer; Dick Immenschuh, construction manager; Kathleen Grady, purchasing brand manager; Bob Waddell, director, purchasing; Brenda Reed, purchasing agent; Shirley Schmitter, design director, Victoria's Secret Stores; Edwin Hofmann, design director, Victoria's Secret Beauty; Tom Stempfley, director, visual presentation, Victoria's Secret Stores; Jane Merriken, vp, visual merchandising, Victoria's Secret Beauty; Marilyn Fong, project management consultant; Kent Colwell, project manager

OUTSIDE DESIGN CONSULTANTS Yabu Pushelberg, Toronto (Victoria's Secret Stores); David Collins, London (Victoria's Secret Beauty); Fisher Development, New York (general contractor); McCall Design Group, San Francisco (production architect); Cooley Monato, New York; Grenald Waldron, Narberth, Pa. (lighting); Anne Baxter, New York (design and materials research)

SUPPLIERS PlayNetwork, Redmond, Wash. (audio); DMX, Seattle, Frog Design, New York (video); Pollack, New York, Kravet, New York, Majilite, Dracut, Mass., Brentano, New York, Designtex, New York (fabrics); Apropos Studio, Minneapolis (architectural coatings); idX, Toronto, LeDan, Mineola, N.Y. (fixturing); Innovative Marble and Tile, Hauppauge, N.Y. (flooring); Living Divani, Milan, Nienkamper, New York, Interior Crafts, Chicago, Galerkin, Gardena, Calif. (furniture); Duggal Photography, New York, Fuel, New York, Studio 212, Phoenix, Amerigraph, Columbus, Ohio, Igloo Color, New York, Skyframe, New York (graphics); Capitol Light, Hartford, Conn. (lighting); Patina-V, City of Industry, Calif. (mannequins); Fusion Specialties, Broomfield, Colo., Greneker, Los Angeles (forms); LeDan, Mineola, N.Y., IDMD, Toronto, Big Apple Signs, Islandia, N.Y., Design Compendium, Brooklyn, N.Y. (props/decoratives); Ruggles, Versailles, Ky. (signage); Maya Romanoff, Chicago, Architectural Systems, New York, Forms+Surfaces, Carpinteria, Calif. (wallcoverings); Silver Threads, Columbus, Ohio (window treatments); Binswanger Glass, Memphis, Tenn. (storefront)

PHOTOGRAPHY © Peter Aaron, Esto Photographics Inc., Mamaroneck, N.Y.; Adrian Wilson, Macclesfield, U.K.

Jacques Despars Kiosk
Galeries de la Capitale, Quebec
GHA Shoppingscapes, Montreal

Canada's Jacques Despars runs 16 full-service hair salons located on the side corridors of malls. To sell its lines of hair care and beauty products, the company decided to install kiosks in the high-traffic main corridors of malls.

GHA Shoppingscapes (Montreal) created a kiosk for Despars that's divided into three main areas: a kidney-shaped island housing cosmetics lines; a U-shaped modular configuration for hair products; and a personal consultation area containing seating and a table. (This area also includes a video/Internet station that Despars beauty consultants can use to provide customers with additional information on the company's products.)

The kiosk's lighting, colors and fixturing suggest the fittings of a luxury spa, offering a refuge for the senses from the surrounding hubbub of the surrounding mall. Four illuminated columns, which descend into and also illuminate the display cases, create a glowing ambience for the kiosk.

Velvety, mint-green coloration, accented with brushed aluminum, etched glass and green gun-metal laminate, highlight the displays. Iridescent, wave-textured vinyl flooring is used as insert panels and paired with a pale green Corian surround.

CLIENT Les Enterprises Jacques, Montreal – Patrice Despars, vp, general director

DESIGN GHA Shoppingscapes, Montreal – Denis Gervais, president; Steve Sutton, vp; Joni Vallon, senior designer; Casey Telefoglou, designer

OUTSIDE DESIGN CONSULTANT Ardoise, Montreal (graphic design)

SUPPLIERS Nemus Ebenisterie, Montreal, Modul-Tech, Montreal (general contractors, fixtures, lighting); Bonaldo, Montreal (furniture); Ardoise, Montreal (graphics); Abet Laminati, Broussard, Que., Arborite, Lasalle, Que., Corian, Montreal (laminates)

PHOTOGRAPHY Yves Lefebvre, Montreal

Place Rosemère Shopping Centre Food Court
Rosemère, Que.

Pappas Design Studio Inc., Montreal

Shopping mall food courts are typically ho-hum affairs, with seating arrangements and surface treatments reminiscent of high-school cafeterias. Owners of the Place Rosemère Shopping Centre in Rosemère, Que., wanted a dining area with a higher level of sophistication, in keeping with the mall's upscale clientele. So, Pappas Design Studio Inc. (Montreal) created a dramatic, contemporary environment featuring 33 skylights, a four-sided stone fireplace and a combination of curvilinear benches and seating counters that delineate clear (and visually interesting) circulation paths.

The outside entrance to the food court is a curved glass facade, accented with mall signage and slat eyebrows that introduces the curved themes found throughout the 650-seat dining area. Similarly, the entrance from the mall features overhead oak slat eye-brows that are repeated toward the corner seating area to create visual balance. To help create a warm, rich environment, many textures – including oak and cherry wood, fabric, metal and wicker – are used in combination throughout the space.

CLIENT Morguard Investments Ltd., Toronto

DESIGN Pappas Design Studio Inc., Montreal – Bess Pappas, principal, Susan Reed

ARCHITECT Petroff Partnership Architects, Markam, Ont.

SUPPLIERS Spinneybeck Leather, North York, Ont., Momentum Textiles, Irvine, Calif. (fabrics); Ceragres, Montreal, Imagine Tile, Bloomfield, N.J. (flooring); Hauser Industries, Waterloo, Ont., Kiosk, Montreal, Groupe SG, Plessisville, Que. (furniture); Pappas Design Studio, Montreal (graphics); Illumination Lighting, Montreal, Lumitech Group, Montreal (lighting); Wilsonart Intl., Temple, Texas (laminates); Media Module, St. Mathias-Sur-Richelieu, Que., Pappas Design Studio, Montreal (signage)

PHOTOGRAPHY Yves Lefebvre, Montreal

Finale
Cambridge, Mass.
Bergmeyer Associates Inc., Boston

While earning their MBAs at Harvard, Paul Conforti and Kim Moore whetted their appetites for their own business, envisioning a high-end dessert and cocktail restaurant that centered on the creative presentation of seasonal gourmet desserts. After researching the market, they put their money where their mouths were and opened Finale in Cambridge, Mass.

Designers from Bergmeyer Associates Inc. (Boston) divided the restaurant into four areas: bakery, bar, main dining room and semi-private dining room. The decor of each space was selected to support the decadent theme of artfully plated desserts. Colors that reference popular dessert ingredients spruce up the dining area, such as yellow walls intended to resemble a mix between butterscotch and crème bruleé. Bittersweet chocolate is referenced through the rich brown color that adorns the millwork and chair-back upholstery, while cherry red carpet and a matching banquette fabric top off the dining room setting.

So that no guests can possibly ignore their sweet tooth, the pastry station was turned into a finishing station in the center of the restaurant, complete with convection oven, refrigerator and worktop area. Mirrors suspended above the station ensure that guests have a clear view of chefs assembling and garnishing the sumptuous desserts.

CLIENT Finale, Cambridge, Mass. – Kim Moore, Paul Conforti, owners

DESIGN AND ARCHITECT Bergmeyer Associates Inc., Boston – Michael Davis, principal-in-charge/project architect; Amy Ballman, designer

GENERAL CONTRACTOR Shawmut Design and Construction, Boston

OUTSIDE DESIGN CONSULTANT Sould Food, Boston (graphic design)

SUPPLIERS Bentley Carpet Mills, Canton, Mass. (flooring); Furniture Concepts, Malden, Mass., Shelby Williams, Morristown, Tenn. (furniture); CX Design, New York, Panoramic Arch Products, Shrewsbury, Mass. (lighting)

PHOTOGRAPHY © Greg Premru, Boston

Max Brenner –
Chocolates by the Bald Man
Sydney

Otto Design Interiors Pty. Ltd., Summer Hill, Australia

In Australia, via Israel, is Max Brenner – Chocolates by the Bald Man, a whimsical name for a serious chocolatier. Max Brenner specializes in chocolate confections and hot chocolate drinks in suckao – a Max Brenner-designed cup with a tealight for heating the chocolate and a metal spoon-straw for drinking.

The company sought an atmosphere that was distinct from the traditional coffee shop when it opened its third location in Australia in November 2002. "It was to be a lot richer and more warm," says Joseph Somma, director/senior designer at Otto Design Interiors Pty. Ltd. (Summer Hill, Australia), "and it needed to have a chocolatey feel to it without actually saying chocolate."

To create this environment, as well as pay tribute to the retailer's handcrafted and handpainted products, designers chose custom-made furniture and warm woods for the ceiling timbers and display cases.

At the counter area, where chocolate drinks and other confections are prepared, an Old World feeling was crafted through the use of vintage ceramic tiles, marble countertops and tarnished copper.

A separate room houses the gift area and "chocolate table" where individual chocolates are sold. Sales associates help customers hand-pick chocolates, which are displayed on custom-made wood trays.

"We have a very concentrated display area to show enough quantity without looking like a supermarket," explains Somma. "Here, the emphasis is on hand-picking."

CLIENT Max Brenner – Chocolates by the Bald Man, Manly Wharf, Sydney

DESIGN Otto Design Interiors Pty. Ltd., Summer Hill, Australia – Joseph Somma, director/senior designer; Mesha Karakashian, Andrea Katehos, design team

GENERAL CONTRACTOR Otto Does Interiors Pty. Ltd., Sydney

SUPPLIERS Otto Does Interiors Pty. Ltd., Sydney (ceilings, fixturing, furniture); Austex, Melbourne (fabrics); Anagote Timbers, Sydney (flooring); Bissanna Tiles, Sydney (tile flooring); Medusa Design, Summer Hill, Australia (graphics); Light Brokers, Homebush, Australia, De de ce, Surry Hills, Australia (lighting); A K Signs, Sydney (signage); Tiletechnics, Sydney (wallcoverings)

PHOTOGRAPHY Jamie Gray, Mona Vale, Sydney

waffle

souf

$4.50

STRAWBERRIES WHITE
CHOCOLATE FLOAT $6.50 FRESH
STRAWBERRIES, WHITE CHOCOLATE
GANACHE, MILK, ICE.

TOFFEE ICE CREAM
CHOCISHAKE $6.50 BROWN SUGAR
TOFFEE, VANILLA CREAM, DARK CHOCOLATE
GANACHE, ICE.

ESPRESSO AND DARK $6.50
TRUFFLE FRAPPE SHOT OF
ESPRESSO, DARK CHOCOLATE GANACHE,
MILK, ICE.

• ICING SUGAR
• STRAWBERRIES
• BANANAS

$2.00 EXTRA
$1.00 EXTRA

WARM CHOCOLATE
FONDUE $6.50
SERVED WITH STRAWBERRIES.

ASSORTMENT OF 6 $11.00
PRALINES

CHOCOLATE LICK $1.50

$3.50

KRYSTAL KUBE

Harris Teeter
Charlotte, N.C.

Little Diversified Architectural Consulting, Charlotte, N.C.

Charlotte's growing urban lifestyle has continued to surge through its hip array of museums, bars, restaurants and condo living. But the young adults and empty nesters made it known that there was a missing link – a full-service grocery store.

Harris Teeter (Matthews, N.C.), the upscale supermarket chain, responded to the need. Because the store was on the street level of a new mid-rise condominium suite, however, designers from Little Diversified Architectural Consulting (Charlotte, N.C.) had to fit a 45,000-square-foot grocery store into an 18,000-square-foot space.

The design team transformed the exterior and interior signage, finishes, decor elements, fixtures, lighting and visual displays to evoke downtown Charlotte's mix of art galleries, banks, restaurants, museums and theaters. Instead of the standard red and green exterior Harris Teeter signage, designers opted for aluminum backlit letters.

The numerous store windows feature minimalistic museum-like displays with plastic white versions of food items such as a milk carton, fruit or ice cream. These red plexi boxes were designed to grab city sidewalkers' attention and to ensure they realize it's a grocery store.

Because designers had to work around massive concrete columns in the middle of the space, fabric wraps were created to conceal them and act as deflectors.

The produce area is subdivided from the rest of the grocery. The department's signage features iridescent vinyl letters that changes from purple to green as you walk by, idea conveying the message that in produce, things change color.

CLIENT Harris Teeter, Matthews, N.C. – Al Lentz, vp, store development; Chris Bond, director, store development; Dean Ochsner, engineering consultant

DESIGN AND ARCHITECT Little Diversified Architectural Consulting, Charlotte, N.C. – Phil Kuttner, ceo; Tim Morrison, principal; Rajeev Bhave, project manager; Daniel Montaño, director of design; Ron Kirkpatrick, project architect; Paige Brice, interior designer

GENERAL CONTRACTOR JB Waddell, Charlotte, N.C.

OUTSIDE DESIGN CONSULTANTS Clive Samuels and Associates, Princeton, N.J. (electrical); Cerami and Associates, New York (acoustical)

SUPPLIERS Madix, Goodwater, Ala. (fixturing); Azrock, Florence, Ala. (flooring); Plastex, Charlotte, N.C. (graphics, signage, props/decoratives); GE Supply, Charlotte, N.C. (lighting); Nevamar, Charlotte, N.C. (laminates); Casco, Kannapolis, N.C. (exterior signage)

PHOTOGRAPHY Tim Buchman, Charlotte, N.C.; Jeffrey Clare Photography, Charlotte, N.C.; Little Diversified Architectural Consulting, Charlotte, N.C.

Shaw's Supermarkets
Prudential Center, Boston
Perennial Inc., Toronto

When Shaw's Supermarkets had the opportunity to open a flagship location in the Prudential Center in downtown Boston, the grocery retailer had a vision not only of a contemporary, urban market, but also of a new model to express its recent efforts in areas like assortment and quality.

The West Bridgewater, Mass.-based supermarket chain, had primarily operated stores in rural and suburban areas. The Boston space is situated among a highly diverse urban population, including both low- and high-income residents, office workers and tourists. The 35,000-square-foot triangular shaped space features a half mezzanine built over the Massachusetts Turnpike, with the opposite side running along Huntington Ave.

The space's 38-foot drum-shaped glass atrium was transformed into the entrance of the Marketfresh Zone, with Shaw's banners artfully suspended from the high ceiling. This entrance brings customers into the produce, deli, seafood, sushi and bakery departments. The Huntington Avenue entrance opens into the "LaCarte" area, Shaw's whole meal replacement

offerings. Windows and large graphics face out onto the sidewalk and let light into the store.

Large billboard graphics in coordinating colors and with raised panels clearly communicate department offerings. The familiar leaf icon in the Shaw's logo was also used as a decorative element on the ceiling.

CLIENT Shaw's Supermarkets, West Bridgewater, Mass. – Steve Lamontagne, Sheryl Frazier, Bob Barry, Joseph Armas, Wayne Macleod, Nadine Lynch

DESIGN Perennial Inc., Toronto – Chris Lund, president and ceo; Jim King, executive vp, co-chief creative officer; Sandra Messore, business manager; Andrew Yeung and Tara O'Neil, directors, environmental design; Steven Comisso, senior designer, environments; Gary Oakley, vp, creative; Sharon Snider, director, design; Michelle Escobar, senior designer, creative; Tom Masters and Victor Sydney, senior production artists

GENERAL CONTRACTOR Lee Kennedy, Boston

ARCHITECT CBT Architects, Boston

SUPPLIERS Tiger Drylac, Ontario, Calif., Armstrong Acoustical Tile, Lancaster, Pa., Gypsum, Chicago (ceilings); Lozier, Omaha, Neb., Interlock Structures, Minneapolis (fixturing); Johnsonite, Chagrin Falls, Ohio, Stonetile Intl., Toronto (flooring); Perennial Inc., Toronto (graphics); Amerlux Lighting Solutions, Fairfield, N.J. (lighting); Pionite, Auburn, Maine, Wilsonart, Temple, Texas, Auralite, Toronto, Formica, Cincinnati, Abet Laminati, Englewood, N.J. (laminates); Don Graves Signs, Walpole, Mass. (signage); Benjamin Moore, Montvale, N.J., Stonetile, Toronto, American Insulated Panel Co., N. Dighton, Mass. (wallcoverings)

PHOTOGRAPHY Richard Johnson, Interior Images, Toronto

Q8 everyday
Nontaburi, Thailand
rkd retail/iQ, Bangkok

Kuwait Petroleum Thailand, operating under the Q8 brand, realized shop performance was the only way to increase market share, brand equity and profit in the future.

The design intent was to maximize exposure and circulation to all product offerings. By angling the upright cooler wall, the traditional "dead corner" was eliminated by bringing this important merchandise category visually closer to the shop entrance. Perpendicular to the wall, the mid-floor gondolas of snack categories are arranged so customers must pass through them on their way to the cooler.

The petroleum industry typically connects the shop component and the pump island into one integrated architectural statement. The new Q8 everyday shop stands independent of the pumps, while the main architectural character is significant in scale as it passes from exterior architecture into interior space.

As a playful reference to the original name play of Q8 from Kuwait, phrases such as Qool Life Style in yellow were developed to identify general merchandise; Fresh and Qool in blue for cold drinks; and Fresh and Quick in orange and magenta for the feature area of ready to heat and eat fast food.

CLIENT Kuwait Petroleum Thailand Ltd., Bangkok – Gerrit Ruitinga, president and managing director; Busaya Tanjasir, marketing development manager

DESIGN AND ARCHITECT rkd retail/iQ, Bangkok – RKurt Durrant, principal-in-charge; Pavin Sethabutra, senior designer; Ratchanee Chaibenjawong, creative director, graphics; Torsak Sursaksilp, graphic designer

GENERAL CONTRACTOR Furline, Bangkok

SUPPLIERS ROL Intl., Samut Prakarn, Thailand (fixturing); Thai Ceramic, Bangkok (flooring); Wilsonart, Bangkok, Thailand (graphics); Lighting & Equipment Co. Ltd., Bangkok (lighting); Perstorp, Bangkok (laminates); Pan Advertising, Bangkok (signage)

PHOTOGRAPHY Pruk Dejuhamhaeng, Bangkok

Spa Nordstrom
Houston Galleria, Houston
Callison Architecture Inc., Seattle

Custom-made furniture and textured, rich material combinations set the tone for a tranquil and luxurious environment at Spa Nordstrom, where the latest body therapies and treatments can be found.

Using a variety of creature comforts to create an enjoyable and indulgent setting, designers at Callison (Seattle) combined highly detailed and textured materials in unusual combinations, such as glass, mica, mother of pearl casework and woven grass panels.

Draperies and translucent art glass panels separate different work spaces throughout the spa, lending privacy to guests and employees.

The spa's earth tone palette is given a feminine touch through the use of soft textures, while artwork and props placed throughout further harmonize the space.

Designers carefully planned for all of the spa equipment to be hidden from guests eyes, adding to a seamless and tranquil setting.

CLIENT Nordstrom, Seattle – Karen Percelle, designer; Nancy Webber, manager of interiors; Bob Vauthier, casework coordinator; Preston Plaxco, project manager; Susan Morton, manager of interiors and casework

DESIGN Callison Architecture Inc., Seattle – M.J. Munsell, principal; Ching Chung, project designer; Dave Brown, design/casework; Sheila May, purchasing; Steve Moody, project manager

GENERAL CONTRACTOR W.E. O'Neil Construction, Chicago

SUPPLIERS Jack Lenor Larsen, New York (drapery); Maharam, Hauppauge, N.Y., Pollack & Associates, New York, Industrial Rubber Supply, Fife, Wash., Great Plains, Chicago, Luna Textiles, San Francisco, Brentano, Northbrook, Ill. (upholstery); Kass Tailored, Mukilteo, Wash., GDM, Paramount, Calif., Hampton Lane, Los Angeles, Waterworks, Seattle, The Mercier Group, Los Angeles, J. Chen, Los Angeles (furniture); J. Chen, Los Angeles, Charles Loomis, Kirkland, Wash., Artemide, Farmingdale, N.Y., Luz Lampcraft, New York (lighting); Peter David, Seattle (art glass); Carnegie, Rockville, N.Y., Evans & Brown, San Francisco (wallcoverings)

PHOTOGRAPHY Chris Eden, Seattle

Mazda
Bountiful, Utah
Design Forum, Dayton, Ohio

Mazda had become known as a car that offered value and Japanese quality but had little personality. The "zoom-zoom" ad campaign was a hit, but did not carry over into the dealership experience. Designers wanted to bring this "zoom-zoom" campaign to life with a focus on design elements that are fast, fun and cool.

The showroom has the feel of a hip garage, balancing fashionable elements with industrial finishes. Raw concrete, corrugated metal, glass, rubber and steel are used throughout the space. Beams and ductwork are exposed, and the mix of industrial and high bay lights mimic typical garage lighting. A large fan provides motion, while an authentic service lift showcases a vehicle high above the space.

Designers introduced bright green and orange to the color palette, supplementing the corporate blue common to many competitors. The exterior features the same bright colors as the interior. Against a backdrop of neon green, passersby see a car featured on the hydraulic lift inside the jewel box windows.

In contrast to the utilitarian look of the showroom, the "m Café" features upscale finishes as well as artifacts of the company's racing heritage. The café offers speed and technology with Internet stations for designing a car, Sony PlayStations to drive an RX-8 and plasma screens showing footage of Mazda's racing success.

CLIENT Mazda, Irvine, Calif. – Charlie Hughes, Jim Hoostal, Bill Ewing, Karen Highberger, Penny Hays, Ross Katz, Dave Sanabria, Dave Tripoli, Ross Fried

DESIGN Design Forum, Dayton, Ohio – Bruce Dybvad, president; Scott Jeffrey, senior vp, planning and design; Jim Williamson, senior vp; John Van Leeuwen, director, space planning development; Scott Chovan, environmental designer

GENERAL CONTRACTOR Cameron Construction, Salt Lake City

ARCHITECT Smith Layton & Associates, Salt Lake City

SUPPLIERS USG, Chicago (ceiling tiles); Prince Street, City of Industry, Calif. (carpet tiles); Shaw Contract, Dalton, Ga. (broadloom carpet); Dal-Tile, Dallas (ceramic tile flooring); EcoSurfaces, Lancaster, Pa. (rubber flooring displays); Endura, Waltham, Mass. (rubber flooring platform); BamStar, Cleveland (bamboo flooring); Keilhauer, Toronto (task/desk/guest seating); Sandler Seating, Atlanta (barstools); Loewenstein, Pompano Beach, Fla. (lounge furniture); Fixtures Furniture, Kansas City, Mo. (kids' furniture); Herman Miller, Zeeland, Mich. (desks/tables/storage); American Custom Lift, La Jolla, Calif. (car lift); Lamin-Art, Schaumburg, Ill., Chemetal, Easthampton, Mass., Formica, Cincinnati, Arborite, Lasalle, Que., Abet Laminati, Englewood, N.J., Pionite, Auburn, Maine (laminates); Corian, Wilmington, Del. (solid surfacing); Atlas, Allentown, Pa. (metal panels); Tnemec, Kansas City, Mo. (paint)

PHOTOGRAPHY Jamie Padgett, Padgett & Co., Chicago

Suzuki Square Retail Image Program
Traverse City, Mich.

Miller Zell Inc., Atlanta

Buying a car can be a stressful, confrontational experi-ence. Suzuki wanted to break that mold by creating a non-threatening, customer-friendly showroom that communicates dealership personnel with nothing to hide. Teaming with Miller Zell Inc. (Atlanta), the automaker came up with the Suzuki Square Retail Image Program, which centers on a clean, clutter-free environment that's designed to encourage open exchanges between buyers and sellers.

The square – as in "square deal" – serves as the cornerstone of the Suzuki brand-image program. The main entrance to the dealership features a large square frame, painted in the brand's signature red and topped with the Suzuki name and logo. (Smaller squares, in different colors, are repeated throughout the dealership's interior as secondary design elements.) A decompression zone, immediately inside the main entrance, is designed to make it easy for customers to identify major dealership departments and also give them a sense of control over their visit.

The showroom's materials palette includes antique white walls to create warmth within the space and a neutral backdrop for vibrant color fixtures; warm-toned woods that serve as visual cues for consultation and reception areas; and rib-textured aluminum that signals customer touch-points.

CLIENT American Suzuki Motor Corp., Brea, Calif. – Koichi Suzuki, assistant to president; Tom Carney, vp, marketing; Chris White, national dealer development; Ken Nishida, retail brand image manager; Chris Moore, dealer development administrator; Suzuki of Traverse City Mich., Dirk Watson, principal

DESIGN Miller Zell Inc., Atlanta – Chip Miller, Bob Holdsworth, account management; Ian Rattray, project director; Lis Diaz, assistant project director; Marty Mahone, creative director; Victoria Lang, designer; Byron Anderson, project manager; Jim Matthews, senior corporate vp, consulting services

GENERAL CONTRACTOR Peninsula Construction, Traverse City, Mich.

ARCHITECT Design Builders, Traverse City Mich.

SUPPLIERS Armstrong World Industries, Lancaster, Pa. (ceilings); Miller Zell Inc., Atlanta (fixturing, graphics); Dal-Tile Corp., Dallas, Shaw Carpet, Atlanta (flooring); Juno Lighting, Des Plaines, Ill., Lithonia, Conyers, Ga., Prisma, Lawrenceville, Ga., Forms + Surfaces, Carpinteria, Calif., io Lighting, Melrose Park, Ill. (lighting); Abet Laminati, Atlanta, Nevamar, Atlanta, Rugby Corp., Atlanta, Pionite, Atlanta (laminates); Coast Sign Inc., Anaheim, Calif. (exterior signage); Eykon, Memphis, Tenn. (wallcoverings)

PHOTOGRAPHY Rion Rizzo, Creative Sources, Atlanta

For more information on visual merchandising and store design, subscribe to:

Books on visual merchandising and store design available from ST Media Group International:

Aesthetics of Merchandise Presentation
Budget Guide to Retail Store Planning & Design
Retail Store Planning & Design Manual
Stores and Retail Spaces
Visual Merchandising
Visual Merchandising and Store Design Workbook

To subscribe, order books or to request a complete catalog of related books and magazines, please contact:

ST Media Group International Inc.
407 Gilbert Avenue
Cincinnati, Ohio 45202

Telephone: 1.800.925.1110 or 513.421.2050
Fax: 513.421.5144 or 513.421.6110
Email: books@stmediagroup.com
Web sites: visualstore (www.visualstore.com) and www.stmediagroup.com